COOKING FOR ONE

Consultant Editor:
Valerie Ferguson

HERMES HOUSE

Contents

Introduction

Cooking for yourself should be pleasant and relaxing. Life can be stressful and hectic, so taking some time to unwind over a favourite dish, attractively served and cooked just the way you like it, is a real pleasure. It is also more satisfying and nutritionally beneficial than relying too often on convenience meals.

Whether you live on your own, have an irregular daily routine from other members of your household, or just prefer different foods, the recipes in this book will provide lots of inspiration. There are ideas for all courses, ranging from substantial suppers to light lunches and snacks, as well as home-made soups, filling vegetarian main courses and melt-in-the-mouth desserts. And, as all the hard work of calculating single portion requirements has already been done for you, there is no waste of excess ingredients or uneaten cooked food.

A helpful introduction offers advice on a healthy diet, specifically with the single person in mind, shopping for one, storing food and getting the most out of the microwave and freezer. Tips throughout the book give further ideas.

It is surprisingly easy to cook for one, so go ahead and enjoy exactly what you like best for every meal.

Basic Nutrition

A healthy diet is one that is varied, so that all the four food groups, as well as essential vitamins and minerals, are included every day.

Starchy Foods

Bread, cereals, pasta, potatoes and rice provide complex carbohydrates, which fuel the body slowly, rather than with a sudden rush of sugar. This group, especially wholegrain foods, such as wholemeal bread, is also an important source of dietary fibre.

Dairy Products

Milk, cheese, yogurt and butter provide protein, vitamins and minerals but may be very high in fats, particularly saturated fats which are thought to raise cholesterol levels in the blood. Eat this group in moderation and consider switching to low-fat dairy products.

Proteins

Meat, fish, poultry, pulses, nuts and eggs supply many vitamins and

Above: Grains are the basis for a wide range of foods, all providing the starch we need for energy.

minerals as well as proteins but some foods also have a high saturated fat content. Eat red meat in moderation. Fish, on the other hand, is often rich in polyunsaturated fats, which may lower levels of blood cholesterol. Skinning chicken before cooking removes almost all the fat. Pulses and nuts are an excellent source of many proteins. Eat eggs in moderation.

Vegetables & Fruit

Some authorities recommend eating five portions from this group each day, as this is thought to help prevent cancer. Raw fruit and vegetables are especially nutritious, providing carbohydrates, minerals and vitamins.

Buying & Storing Food

A well-stocked kitchen makes preparing meals easy and the key is planning. Plan your menus for the next few days or even the week ahead and make a shopping list that includes both fresh foods and stock items that are running low or near to their use-by dates.

Perishable foods, such as butter, milk, cheese, meat and fish, should be stored in the refrigerator. Cover food or put it into rigid plastic containers. This preserves flavour and moisture and prevents odours of strong foods being transferred. Raw meat and poultry should be wrapped and placed where no drips can contaminate other food. Ripe fruits and perishable vegetables should be stored in the salad drawer. The temperature should be 1–5°C/34–41°F.

Root vegetables, such as carrots, potatoes and onions, are best stored in a cool, dark place, preferably in a rack where the air can circulate. Never store them in plastic as they will rot.

The Freezer

A small freezer can be invaluable for storing both leftovers and fresh foods. Special offers in supermarkets often entail buying more than is required for one meal, such as four chicken pieces. You can either freeze three of them individually to be prepared on other occasions or cook your favourite chicken dish and freeze three separate portions. Leftovers must be allowed to cool completely and then transferred to the freezer. Food should always be packed in rigid containers or wrapped in foil, two layers of clear film or plastic freezer bags.

The Microwave

The microwave is a very economical way of cooking because it is so rapid, whereas heating an entire conventional oven for a single serving is rather more extravagant. Always follow the manufacturer's instructions, including standing time, which is an integral part of cooking in the microwave. Never put anything metal in the microwave, except a shelf supplied by the manufacturer with the oven. Use microwave-proof containers and do not cover dishes with foil. Most casseroles and stews, many soups and baked dishes cook well in the microwave.

The microwave is also ideal for defrosting frozen foods quickly, although not all are suitable. Again, follow the manufacturer's instructions and remember to remove any foil.

Above: Vegetables, especially raw, are rich in vitamins and fibre.

The Store Cupboard

Stock this sensibly and you'll always have the wherewithal to make a tasty, satisfying meal. Begin with the basics and expand as you experiment, buying small quantities and keeping an eye on use-by dates.

Canned Vegetables & Pulses

Although fresh vegetables are best for most cooking, canned varieties are convenient, quick to use and usually available in small quantities. Popular and useful canned vegetables include artichoke hearts for livening up stir-fries, salads, risottos and pizzas, pimientos for flavouring stews and soups and sweetcorn for colour and crunchiness. Canned pulses are great time-savers as they do not require soaking or prolonged cooking. Chick-peas, cannellini beans, green lentils, haricot beans and red kidney beans all survive the canning process well. Rinse canned pulses in cold running water and drain well before use.

Above: A well-stocked store cupboard is an essential for the busy cook.

Cereals

Rice is a staple for over half the world and immensely useful. If you stock only one type, make it basmati, which has a superior flavour and fragrance. A mixture of basmati and wild rice works well. Dried pasta cooks in about 10 minutes and goes with almost everything, from vegetables to cheese and from meat to fish. Spaghetti and, perhaps, one chunky shape such as penne will go with most sauces. It is well worth stocking some Chinese noodles to serve with stir-fries and other Chinese dishes.

Cooking & Salad Oils

Groundnut oil is inexpensive and bland-tasting so it will not mask delicate flavours. It is a good, all-purpose cooking oil, but you could also use vegetable or sunflower oil. Olive oil is good for most purposes, except deep-frying, and extra virgin olive oil is perfect for salad dressings. Other popular oils include sesame, used for flavouring Chinese and Asian dishes, and chilli oil which adds instant and fiery spice to stir-fries and vegetables.

Herbs & Spices

Always buy dried herbs and spices in small quantities and keep well sealed as they can go stale and flavourless very quickly. Useful basic dried herbs include bay leaves, marjoram or oregano, mint, rosemary and thyme. Some fresh herbs, such as coriander, store best frozen in ice cube trays. Commercial pesto is a good substitute for fresh basil. One or two small pots of growing herbs, such as parsley and chives, add flavour to food and cheer up the kitchen. Useful basic spices include Chinese five-spice powder, coriander, cumin, nutmeg and turmeric. Freshly ground spices have more flavour and freshly ground black pepper is a must.

Other Flavourings

If you like Chinese food, it is worth buying a bottle of good-quality soy sauce to flavour stir-fries. Dijon mustard, chilli sauce and tahini are useful for many dishes.

Tomatoes

Canned tomatoes are a multi-purpose store-cupboard standby. Available whole or chopped, plain or with herbs, spices and other flavouring, they can be added to soups, stews, casseroles and pasta sauces. Tomato purée, a concentrated tomato paste sold in tubes, cans and jars, imparts an instant tomato flavour to many dishes. A sun-dried version is also available. Passata is a thick sauce made from sieved tomatoes, also used to add a concentrated tomato flavour. Sun-dried tomatoes are available in bags or in jars of oil. The oil may be used in cooked dishes and salad dressings for a strong tomato flavour.

Above: A selection of oils, vinegars and flavourings to add interest to your dishes.

Fresh Tomato Soup

Served hot or chilled, this fresh-tasting soup is easy to prepare.

Serves 1

INGREDIENTS
250 g/9 oz ripe tomatoes
60 ml/4 tbsp chicken or vegetable stock
7.5 ml/1½ tsp sun-dried tomato paste
5–7.5 ml/1–1½ tsp balsamic vinegar
pinch of caster sugar
5 ml/1 tsp fresh basil leaves
salt and freshly ground black pepper
fresh basil leaves, to garnish
toasted cheese croûtes and crème fraîche,
   to serve

1 Plunge the tomatoes into boiling water for 30 seconds, then refresh in cold water. Peel away the skins and quarter the tomatoes. Put them in a large saucepan and pour over the chicken or vegetable stock.

2 Bring to the boil, reduce the heat, cover and simmer for 10 minutes until the tomatoes are pulpy.

3 Stir in the tomato paste, vinegar, sugar and basil. Season with salt and pepper, then cook gently, stirring, for a further 2 minutes.

4 Process the soup in a blender or food processor, then return to the pan and reheat gently. Serve topped with one or two toasted cheese croûtes and a spoonful of crème fraîche, garnished with basil leaves.

COOK'S TIP: To make cheese croûtes, toast slices of French bread sprinkled with Parmesan.

Thai-style Chicken Soup

Coconut milk, lemon grass, ginger and lime make a fragrant soup.

Serves 1

INGREDIENTS
5 ml/1 tsp vegetable oil
1 small fresh red chilli, seeded and chopped
1 garlic clove, crushed
1 small leek, thinly sliced
150 ml/¼ pint/⅔ cup chicken stock
105 ml/7 tbsp coconut milk
1–2 boneless, skinless chicken thighs, cut
    into bite-size pieces
7.5 ml/1½ tsp Thai fish sauce
½ lemon grass stalk
1.5 ml/¼ tsp finely chopped fresh root ginger
pinch of sugar
1 kaffir lime leaf (optional)
60 ml/4 tbsp frozen peas, thawed
10 ml/2 tsp chopped fresh coriander

1 Heat the oil in a large saucepan and cook the chilli and garlic for about 2 minutes. Add the leek and cook for a further 2 minutes.

2 Stir in the chicken stock and coconut milk and bring to the boil over a medium heat.

3 Add the chicken, with the fish sauce, lemon grass, ginger, sugar and lime leaf, if using. Simmer, covered, for 15 minutes or until the chicken is tender, stirring occasionally.

4 Add the peas and cook for a further 3 minutes. Remove the lemon grass. Stir in the coriander before serving.

Courgette Soup with Small Pasta Shapes

The pasta makes this quite a substantial soup which, served with crusty bread and cheese, would make a meal in itself.

Serves 1

INGREDIENTS
15 ml/1 tbsp olive or
    sunflower oil
1 small onion, finely chopped
350 ml/12 fl oz/1½ cups
    chicken stock
225 g/8 oz courgettes
60 ml/4 tbsp small soup pasta
lemon juice
salt and freshly ground
    black pepper
10 ml/2 tsp chopped
    fresh chervil
soured cream, to garnish

2 Meanwhile, grate the courgettes and stir into the boiling stock with the pasta. Turn down the heat and simmer for 10 minutes, until the pasta is tender. Season to taste with lemon juice, salt and pepper.

3 Stir in the chervil and add a swirl of soured cream before serving.

VARIATION: This attractive, summery soup can be made with cucumber if courgettes are unavailable. In this case, use chopped fennel, tarragon or dill instead of chervil.

1 Heat the oil in a large saucepan and add the onion. Cover and cook gently for about 20 minutes until very soft but not coloured, stirring occasionally. Add the stock and bring to the boil.

COOK'S TIP: If you don't have any fresh stock, use good-quality canned chicken or beef consommé instead of a stock cube.

Mussels Steamed in White Wine

This classic French dish is simple to prepare. Serve with plenty of crusty French bread to mop up the juices.

Serves 1

INGREDIENTS
500 g/1¼ lb fresh mussels
75 ml/5 tbsp dry
    white wine
1 large shallot, finely chopped
bouquet garni
freshly ground
    black pepper

2 In a heavy flameproof casserole, combine the wine, shallot, bouquet garni and plenty of pepper. Bring to the boil over a medium-high heat and cook for 2 minutes.

1 Discard any broken mussels and those with open shells that refuse to close when tapped. Under cold running water, scrape the mussel shells with a knife to remove any barnacles and pull out the stringy "beards". Soak the mussels in several changes of cold water for at least 1 hour.

COOK'S TIP: For Mussels with Cream Sauce, cook as above, but transfer the mussels to a warmed bowl and cover to keep warm. Strain the cooking liquid through a muslin-lined sieve into a large saucepan and boil for about 7–10 minutes to reduce by half. Stir in 20 ml/4 tsp whipping cream and 7.5 ml/1½ tsp chopped parsley, then add the mussels. Cook for about 1 minute more to reheat the mussels.

3 Add the mussels and cook, tightly covered, for 5 minutes, or until the mussels open, shaking and tossing the pan occasionally. Discard any mussels that do not open.

4 Using a slotted spoon, transfer the mussels to a warmed soup plate. Tilt the casserole a little and hold for a few seconds to allow any sand to settle in the bottom. Spoon or pour the cooking liquid over the mussels, then serve at once with crusty French bread.

VARIATION: Instead of white wine, use the same amount of dry cider. If you prefer a thicker sauce, stir an egg yolk into the cooking liquid before pouring it over the mussels.

Marinated Mixed Vegetables with Basil Oil

Basil oil is a must for drizzling over plain stir-fried vegetables. It will keep in the fridge for up to two weeks.

Serves 1

INGREDIENTS
7.5 ml/1½ tsp olive oil
1 garlic clove, crushed
rind of ½ lemon, finely grated
1 x 200 g/7 oz can artichoke
   hearts, drained
1 large leek, sliced
115 g/4 oz patty pan squash,
   halved, if large
1 large plum tomato, cut into
   segments lengthways
15 g/½ oz fresh basil leaves
150 ml/¼ pint/⅔ cup extra virgin
   olive oil
salt and freshly ground
   black pepper

2 Place the artichokes, leek, patty pan squash and plum tomato in a large bowl, pour over the marinade and leave for 30 minutes.

3 Meanwhile, make the basil oil. Blend the fresh basil leaves with the extra virgin olive oil in a food processor until puréed, pushing down a couple of times with a spatula.

1 Thoroughly mix together the olive oil, garlic and lemon rind in a bowl, to make a marinade.

4 Heat a wok, then stir-fry the marinated vegetables for 3–4 minutes, tossing well. Drizzle basil oil over the vegetables and serve.

Chicken Liver & Bacon Salad

Warm salads, with their interesting combination of hot and cold elements, are becoming increasingly popular.

Serves 1

INGREDIENTS

50 g/2 oz young spinach,
  stems removed
¼ frisée lettuce
30 ml/2 tbsp groundnut or
  sunflower oil
1–2 thick slices rindless unsmoked back
  bacon, cut into strips
1 slice day-old bread, crusts removed and
  cut into short fingers
115 g/4 oz chicken livers
5 cherry tomatoes
salt and freshly ground
  black pepper

1 Place the salad leaves in a bowl. Heat half the oil in a large frying pan. Add the bacon and cook for 3–4 minutes, or until crisp and brown. Remove with a slotted spoon and drain on kitchen paper.

2 To make the croûtons, fry the bread in the bacon-flavoured oil until crisp and golden. Drain on kitchen paper.

3 Heat the remaining oil, add the chicken livers and fry briskly for 2–3 minutes. Place the livers on the salad leaves, and add the bacon, croûtons and tomatoes. Season, toss and serve.

Pear with Stilton

This is a classic British starter, but it also makes an easy and filling snack at any time of day.

Serves 1

INGREDIENTS
1 ripe pear, slightly chilled
25 g/1 oz blue Stilton cheese
15 ml/1 tbsp curd cheese
freshly ground
   black pepper
watercress sprigs, to garnish

FOR THE DRESSING
15 ml/1 tbsp olive oil
5 ml/1 tsp lemon juice
7.5 ml/1½ tsp toasted
   poppy seeds
salt and freshly ground
   black pepper

1 First make the dressing: place the olive oil, lemon juice, poppy seeds and seasoning in a screw-topped jar and shake together until emulsified.

2 Cut the pear in half lengthways, then scoop out the core and cut away the calyx from the rounded end.

3 Beat together the Stilton, curd cheese and a little pepper. Divide this mixture evenly between the cavities in the pear halves.

4 Shake the dressing to mix it again, then spoon it over the pear. Serve garnished with watercress.

Salmon with Yogurt & Mint Dressing

Salmon is a very rich fish and is delicious grilled and served with this light and delicate sauce.

Serves 1

INGREDIENTS
10 cm/4 in piece cucumber
6 fresh mint leaves
150 ml/¼ pint/⅔ cup natural
   Greek yogurt
175 g/6 oz salmon fillet, scaled
olive oil, for brushing
salt and freshly ground black pepper
mint sprigs, to garnish
fresh spinach leaves,
   to serve

3 Chop the mint leaves. Place the chopped mint leaves in a bowl with the yogurt.

1 Peel the cucumber, slice in half lengthways and remove the seeds.

2 Grate the cucumber into a sieve, salt lightly and drain for about 5 minutes.

4 Squeeze out any excess juice from the cucumber and stir into the bowl with the yogurt and mint. Season with black pepper and set aside. Preheat the grill until moderately hot.

COOK'S TIP: Cover and store any leftover yogurt and mint dressing in the fridge. You can serve it with plain lamb chops the following day.

5 Brush the salmon with olive oil and season with a little salt. Grill for 3 minutes, skin side up, then carefully turn it over and grill for about 2 minutes on the other side. The skin should be browned and crisp.

6 Serve on a bed of spinach with the yogurt and cucumber dressing. Garnish with mint and sprinkle over some freshly ground black pepper.

21

Smoked Haddock Fillet with Quick Parsley Sauce

Make any herb sauce with this method, making sure it is thickened and seasoned well to complement the smoky flavour of the fish.

Serves 1

INGREDIENTS
225 g/8 oz smoked haddock fillet
25 g/1 oz/2 tbsp butter, softened
30 ml/2 tbsp plain flour
150 ml/¼ pint/⅔ cup milk
15–30 ml/1–2 tbsp chopped fresh parsley,
   plus extra, to garnish
salt and freshly ground black pepper

1 Smear the fish fillet on both sides with half the butter and preheat the grill until moderately hot.

2 Beat the remaining butter and flour together in a bowl to make a paste.

3 Grill the fish for 10–15 minutes, turning when necessary. Meanwhile, heat the milk until just below boiling point. Add the flour mixture in small knobs, whisking constantly over the heat. Continue until the sauce is smooth and thick.

4 Stir in the seasoning and parsley and serve poured over the fish garnished with parsley.

Tuna with Coriander Crust & Mango Salsa

Fresh tuna is very meaty and filling and is perfectly matched with a fruity salsa that takes only moments to make.

Serves 1

INGREDIENTS
finely grated rind of ¼ lemon
1.5 ml/¼ tsp black peppercorns
15 ml/1 tbsp finely
    chopped onion
7.5 ml/1½ tsp chopped
    fresh coriander
175 g/6 oz fresh tuna steak
30 ml/2 tbsp olive oil

FOR THE SALSA
¼ mango, peeled and diced
15 ml/1 tbsp lime juice
5 ml/1 tsp grated lime rind
¼ red chilli, seeded and
    finely chopped

1 First, make the salsa. Mix the mango, lime juice, rind and chilli in a bowl and marinate for at least 1 hour.

2 Mix together the lemon rind, black peppercorns, onion and coriander in a coffee grinder to make a coarse paste.

3 Spread this on one side of the steak with the flat side of a knife.

4 Heat the olive oil in a heavy-based frying pan until it begins to smoke. Add the tuna, paste-side down, and fry until a crust forms. Lower the heat and turn the steak to cook for one minute. Pat off excess oil with kitchen paper. Serve with mango salsa.

Red Snapper with Herb Salsa

This simple dish is delicious served with mixed salad leaves, garnished with coriander and curls of orange rind.

Serves 1

INGREDIENTS
175 g/6 oz snapper fillet
5 ml/1 tsp vegetable oil
10 g/¼ oz butter
salt and freshly ground black pepper

FOR THE SALSA
15 g/½ oz fresh coriander or
   parsley leaves
120 ml/4 fl oz/½ cup olive oil
1 garlic clove, chopped
1 small tomato, cored and chopped
7.5 ml/1½ tsp fresh orange juice
5 ml/1 tsp sherry vinegar
pinch of salt

2 Transfer to a bowl. Stir in the orange juice, vinegar and salt. Set the salsa aside. Rinse the fish and pat dry. Sprinkle with salt and pepper.

3 Heat the oil and butter in a large non-stick frying pan. When hot, add the fish and cook for 2–3 minutes until the flesh is opaque.

1 First make the salsa. Place the coriander or parsley, oil and garlic in a food processor or blender. Process until almost smooth. Add the tomato and pulse on and off several times; the mixture should be slightly chunky.

4 Carefully transfer the fish to a warmed dinner plate using a fish slice or wide spatula. Top with a spoonful of salsa. Serve additional salsa on the side.

Plaice & Pesto Parcel

Wrapping the fish in a parcel helps to keep it moist during cooking.

Serves 1

INGREDIENTS
25 g/1 oz/2 tbsp butter
5 ml/1 tsp pesto sauce
2 small plaice fillets
¼ small fennel bulb, cut into matchsticks
1 small carrot, cut into matchsticks
1 small courgette, cut into matchsticks
2.5 ml/½ tsp finely grated lemon rind
sunflower oil, for brushing
salt and freshly ground black pepper
fresh basil leaves, to garnish

1 Preheat the oven to 190°C/375°F/ Gas 5. Beat half the butter with the pesto and seasoning to taste. Skin the fillets, then spread the pesto butter over the skinned side and roll up, starting from the thick end.

2 Melt the remaining butter in a pan. Add the fennel and carrot and sauté for 3 minutes. Add the courgette and cook for 2 minutes. Remove from the heat. Add the lemon rind and season.

3 Oil a square of greaseproof paper. Spoon the vegetables into the centre, then place the rolls on top. Seal the parcel and place in a roasting tin. Bake for 15–20 minutes. Open up the parcel and sprinkle with the basil.

Skate with Lemon

Lemon and capers are classic partners for fish.

Serves 1

INGREDIENTS
1 small skate wing, about 175–225 g/6–8 oz
seasoned plain flour
22.5 ml/4½ tsp olive oil
1 garlic clove, crushed
5 ml/1 tsp finely grated lemon rind
30 ml/2 tbsp lemon juice
7.5 ml/1½ tsp capers, rinsed, drained and chopped
7.5 ml/1½ tsp chopped fresh flat leaf parsley
5 ml/1 tsp chopped fresh basil
5 ml/1 tsp snipped fresh chives
salt and freshly ground black pepper

1 Lightly dust the skate in the seasoned flour. Heat 7.5 ml/1½ tsp of the oil in a large frying pan and, when hot, add the skate and fry for 8–10 minutes, turning once.

2 Meanwhile, mix together the remaining oil, the garlic, lemon rind and juice in a bowl with the capers, parsley, basil, chives and seasoning.

3 Pour the sauce into a pan to warm through. Serve the skate with the sauce spooned over the top.

Right: Plaice & Pesto Parcel (top); Skate with Lemon

Mediterranean Prawns

Skewered prawns make a delicious summer supper dish.

Serves 1

INGREDIENTS
4 raw king prawns, peeled
1 garlic clove, finely chopped
20 ml/4 tsp finely chopped fresh parsley
1 small fresh rosemary sprig, leaves removed
   and finely chopped
pinch of dried chilli flakes
45ml/3 tbsp fresh lime juice
7.5 ml/1½ tsp olive oil
salt and freshly ground black pepper
green salad, to serve

1 Remove the black thread that runs along the back of the prawns. Make cuts along the back, without cutting through, then carefully fan out.

2 Blend the garlic, herbs, chilli flakes, lime juice, oil and seasoning in a bowl. Add the prawns, stir well and marinate for 1 hour. Soak four wooden skewers in warm water for at least 30 minutes.

3 Preheat the grill until very hot. Thread two prawns on to each pair of skewers and grill for 2–3 minutes. Remove the prawns from the skewers and serve with green salad.

Right: Mediterranean Prawns (top);
Scallops with Lemon & Thyme

Scallops with Lemon & Thyme

If using the shell, make sure it is well scrubbed first.

Serves 1

INGREDIENTS
15 ml/1 tbsp olive oil
1 garlic clove, finely chopped
leaves from 1 fresh thyme sprig
1 small bay leaf
5 ml/1 tsp chopped fresh parsley
4 fresh scallops, rinsed
½ small shallot, finely chopped
5 ml/1 tsp balsamic vinegar
7.5 ml/1½ tsp lemon juice
30 ml/2 tbsp chicken or vegetable stock
salt and freshly ground
   black pepper
6 baby spinach leaves, to garnish

1 Blend the olive oil, garlic, thyme, bay leaf and parsley in a bowl. Add the scallops and marinate for 1 hour. Heat a heavy-based frying pan. Remove the scallops from the marinade and sear for about 30 seconds on each side. Transfer to a plate and keep warm.

2 Add the marinade to the pan with the shallot, balsamic vinegar, lemon juice and stock. Cook over a high heat for 2–3 minutes, until the stock is well reduced. Discard the bay leaf and season. Arrange the spinach leaves on a serving plate, place the scallops in the shell and pour over the juices.

Chicken with Tomatoes & Olives

Chicken breasts or turkey, veal or pork escalopes may be flattened for quick and even cooking.

Serves 1

INGREDIENTS
150–175 g/5–6 oz skinless, boneless
    chicken breast
pinch of cayenne pepper
22.5 ml/4½ tsp extra virgin
    olive oil
1 garlic clove,
    finely chopped
15 black olives
2 plum tomatoes, chopped
15 ml/1 tbsp fresh basil leaves
salt

1 Carefully remove the fillet (the long finger-shaped muscle on the back of the breast) and reserve for another use.

2 Place the chicken breast between two sheets of greaseproof paper or clear film and pound with the flat side of a meat mallet or roll out with a rolling pin to flatten to about 1cm /½ in thick. Season with salt and cayenne pepper.

COOK'S TIP: If the tomato skins are tough, remove them by scoring the base of each tomato with a knife, then plunging them into boiling water for 30 seconds. The skin should simply peel off.

3 Heat 15 ml/1 tbsp of the olive oil in a large frying pan over a medium-high heat. Add the chicken and cook for 4–5 minutes, until golden brown and just cooked, turning it once. Transfer the chicken to a warmed serving plate and keep warm.

4 Wipe out the frying pan and return to the heat. Add the remaining olive oil and fry the garlic for 1 minute, until golden and fragrant. Stir in the olives, cook for a further 1 minute, then stir in the tomatoes.

5 Shred the basil leaves and stir into the olive and tomato mixture, then spoon it over the chicken and serve.

Chicken & Coriander with Mangetouts

Stir-fries are probably the original fast food, taking only minutes to cook and tasting utterly wonderful.

Serves 1

INGREDIENTS
1 skinless, boneless chicken breast
50 g/2 oz mangetouts
15 ml/1 tbsp vegetable oil, plus extra for
    deep-frying
1 garlic clove, finely chopped
5 ml/1 tsp grated fresh root ginger
2 spring onions, cut into
    4 cm/1½ in lengths
2.5 ml/½ tsp sesame oil
15 ml/1 tbsp chopped fresh coriander
boiled rice, to serve

FOR THE MARINADE
1.5 ml/¼ tsp cornflour
5 ml/1 tsp light soy sauce
5 ml/1 tsp medium dry sherry
5 ml/1 tsp vegetable oil

FOR THE SAUCE
1.5 ml/¼ tsp cornflour
5 ml/1 tsp dark soy sauce
30 ml/2 tbsp chicken stock
5 ml/1 tsp oyster sauce

1 Cut the chicken into strips about 1 x 4 cm/½ x 1½ in. To make the marinade, blend together the cornflour and soy sauce. Stir in the sherry and oil. Pour over the chicken pieces, and leave for 30 minutes.

2 Trim the mangetouts and plunge into a pan of boiling salted water. Bring back to the boil, then drain and refresh them under cold running water. Drain again.

3 To make the sauce, mix together the cornflour, soy sauce, stock and oyster sauce and set aside.

4 Heat the oil in a deep-fryer. Drain the chicken strips and fry for about 30 seconds to brown. Drain and transfer to a plate, with a slotted spoon.

5 Heat half the vegetable oil in a preheated wok and add the garlic and ginger. Stir-fry for 30 seconds. Add the mangetouts and stir-fry for a further 1–2 minutes. Transfer to a plate and keep warm.

6 Heat the remaining vegetable oil in the wok, add the spring onions and stir-fry for 1–2 minutes. Add the chicken and stir-fry for 2 minutes. Pour in the sauce, reduce the heat and cook for 4 minutes, until it thickens and the chicken is cooked through.

7 Stir the sesame oil into the chicken mixture. Serve with fresh boiled rice, and top with the mangetouts. Sprinkle with chopped fresh coriander.

Duck Breast with Pineapple & Ginger

Boneless duck breast is available from most supermarkets and makes a substantial meal for one.

Serves 1

INGREDIENTS
1 boneless duck breast
2 spring onions, chopped
7.5 ml/1½ tsp light soy sauce
115 g/4 oz can pineapple rings
20 ml/4 tsp water
1 piece drained Chinese stem ginger in
   syrup, plus 10 ml/2 tsp syrup from the jar
7.5 ml/1½ tsp cornflour, mixed to a thin
   paste with a little water
salt and freshly ground black pepper
egg noodles, baby spinach and
   green beans, to serve
15 ml/1 tbsp strips green pepper,
   to garnish
15 ml/1 tbsp strips red pepper, to garnish

1 Carefully remove the skin from the duck breast. Select a shallow bowl that will fit into your steamer and that will accommodate the duck breast. Spread out the chopped spring onions in the bowl, arrange the duck breast on top and cover with non-stick baking paper.

2 Set the steamer over boiling water and cook the duck breast for about 1 hour, or until it is tender. Remove the duck breast from the steamer and leave until it is cool enough to handle.

3 Cut the duck into thin slices. Place on a plate and moisten with a little of the cooking juices from the steaming bowl. Strain the remaining juices into a saucepan with the soy sauce and set aside. Cover the duck slices with the baking paper or foil and keep warm.

4 Drain the canned pineapple rings, reserving 15 ml/1 tbsp of the juice. Add this to the reserved cooking juices in the pan, together with the measured water. Stir in the ginger syrup, then stir in the cornflour paste and cook, stirring, until thickened. Season to taste.

5 Cut the pineapple and ginger into attractive shapes. Put the cooked noodles, baby spinach and green beans on a plate, add slices of duck and top with the pineapple, ginger and pepper strips. Pour over the sauce and serve.

Braised Ham with Madeira Sauce

With very little effort or expense, you can transform an unexciting ham steak into an elegant gourmet dish.

Serves 1

INGREDIENTS
25 g/1 oz/2 tbsp unsalted butter
1 shallot, finely chopped
7.5 ml/1½ tsp plain flour
5 ml/1 tsp tomato purée
120 ml/4 fl oz/½ cup beef stock
22.5 ml/4½ tsp Madeira
175–200 g/6–7 oz ham steak
salt and freshly ground black pepper
watercress, to garnish
creamed potatoes, to serve

2 Sprinkle over the flour and cook for 3–4 minutes, until well browned, stirring constantly, then whisk in the tomato purée and stock and season with pepper. Simmer over a low heat until the sauce is reduced by about half, stirring occasionally.

3 Taste the sauce and adjust the seasoning, then stir in the Madeira and cook for 2–3 minutes.

1 Melt half the butter in a medium-size saucepan over a medium-high heat, then add the shallot and cook for 2–3 minutes, until just softened, stirring frequently.

COOK'S TIP: To make the sauce a deeper colour, add a few drops of gravy browning to the stock.

4 Strain into a small bowl and keep warm in a low oven or over a saucepan of just simmering water.

5 Snip the edges of the ham steak to prevent it curling. Melt the remaining butter in a large frying pan over a medium-high heat, then add the ham steak and cook for 4–5 minutes or until cooked through, turning once. Transfer the ham to a warmed plate and pour over the sauce. Garnish with watercress and serve with creamed potatoes.

37

Lamb Chops with Mint

The classic combination is here given a slightly unusual twist.

Serves 1

INGREDIENTS

2 loin lamb chops or 1 double loin
    lamb chop, about 2 cm/¾ in thick
coarsely ground black pepper
fresh mint, to garnish
sautéed potatoes, to serve

FOR THE MINT VINAIGRETTE

7.5 ml/1½ tsp white wine vinegar
1.5 ml/¼ tsp clear honey
1 small garlic clove, very
    finely chopped
15 ml/1 tbsp extra virgin
    olive oil
15 ml/1 tbsp finely chopped
    fresh mint
1 small tomato, peeled, seeded and
    finely diced
salt and freshly ground black pepper

1 First, make the vinaigrette. Put the vinegar, honey, garlic, salt and pepper in a small bowl and whisk thoroughly to combine. Slowly whisk in the oil, then stir in the mint and tomato and set aside for up to 1 hour.

2 Put the lamb chops on a board and trim off any excess fat. Sprinkle with the pepper and press on to both sides of the meat, coating it evenly.

3 Lightly oil a cast iron griddle and set over a high heat until very hot, but not smoking. Place the chops on the griddle and reduce the heat to medium. Cook the chops for 6–7 minutes, turning once, or until done as preferred. Serve the chops with the vinaigrette and the sautéed potatoes, garnished with mint.

Peppered Steak in Beer

Robust flavours for a hearty appetite. Serve with salad and jacket potatoes.

Serves 1

INGREDIENTS
175 g/6 oz beef sirloin or rump steak,
   about 2.5 cm/1 in thick
1 garlic clove, crushed
30 ml/2 tbsp brown ale or stout
7.5 ml/1½ tsp dark muscovado sugar
7.5 ml/1½ tsp Worcestershire sauce
5 ml/1 tsp corn oil
5 ml/1 tsp crushed black peppercorns

1 Place the steak in a deep dish and add the garlic, ale or stout, sugar, Worcestershire sauce and oil. Turn to coat evenly in the marinade, and then leave to marinate in the fridge for 2–3 hours or overnight.

2 Remove the steak from the dish and reserve the marinade. Sprinkle the peppercorns over the steak and press them into the surface. Preheat the grill.

3 Cook the steak under a hot grill, basting it occasionally with the reserved marinade during cooking.

4 Turn the steak once during cooking and cook it for 3–6 minutes on each side, depending on how rare you like it.

COOK'S TIP: Take care when basting with the marinade, spoon on just a small amount at a time.

Chilli Beef with Basil

This is a dish for chilli lovers! It is very easy to prepare and cook.

Serves 1

INGREDIENTS
about 45 ml/3 tbsp groundnut oil
8–10 large fresh basil leaves
150 g/5 oz rump steak
15 ml/1 tbsp Thai fish sauce
2.5 ml/½ tsp dark soft
   brown sugar
1 fresh red chilli, sliced into rings
1 garlic clove, chopped
2.5 ml/½ tsp chopped fresh
   root ginger
1 small shallot, thinly sliced
15 ml/1 tbsp chopped fresh
   basil leaves
dash of lemon juice
salt and freshly ground
   black pepper
boiled rice, to serve

2 Cut the steak across the grain into thin strips. In a bowl, mix together the fish sauce and sugar. Add the beef, mix well, then leave to marinate for about 30 minutes.

3 Reheat the oil until hot, add the chilli, garlic, ginger and shallot and stir-fry for 30 seconds. Add the beef and chopped basil, then stir-fry for about 3 minutes. Flavour with lemon juice and add seasoning to taste.

1 Heat the oil in a preheated wok and, when hot, add the whole basil leaves and fry for about 1 minute, until crisp. Drain on kitchen paper. Remove the wok from the heat and pour off all but 15 ml/1 tbsp of the oil.

COOK'S TIP: To reduce the heat of the chilli, remove the seeds before cooking. Wash your hands carefully after handling cut chillies.

4 Transfer to a warmed serving plate, scatter over the fried basil leaves and serve immediately with boiled rice.

Red Pepper Stuffed with Minced Beef

This easy all-in-one dish may be cooked in a conventional oven or, for speed and economy, in the microwave.

Serves 1

INGREDIENTS
1 red pepper
½ small onion
1 celery stick
115 g/4 oz/1 cup minced beef
15 ml/1 tbsp olive oil
2–3 button mushrooms
pinch of ground cinnamon
salt and freshly ground
   black pepper
flat leaf parsley, to garnish
green salad, to serve

1 Cut the top off the red pepper and reserve it. Remove the seeds and membranes from the pepper.

2 Finely chop the onion and celery. Set aside. Sauté the minced beef in a non-stick frying pan for a few minutes, stirring until it is no longer red. Transfer to a plate.

3 Pour half the oil into the frying pan and sauté the chopped vegetables over high heat until the onion starts to brown. Add the mushrooms and stir in the partly cooked beef. Season with the cinnamon, salt and pepper. Cook over low heat for 15 minutes.

4 Preheat the oven to 190°C/375°F/ Gas 5. Cut a sliver off the base of the pepper so it stands level, spoon in the beef mixture, replace the lid. Place in an oiled dish, drizzle over the remaining oil and cook for 20 minutes. Garnish with parsley. Serve with green salad.

VARIATION: You could use minced lamb for this dish instead of beef, if you prefer.

Balti Stir-fried Vegetables with Cashew Nuts

This versatile stir-fry will accommodate most other combinations of vegetables – you do not have to use the selection suggested here.

Serves 1

INGREDIENTS
1 small carrot
½ small red pepper, seeded
½ small green pepper, seeded
1 small courgette
25 g/1 oz green beans
1–2 spring onions
5 ml/1 tsp extra virgin olive oil
1 curry leaf
pinch of white cumin seeds
1 dried red chilli, chopped
15 ml/1 tbsp cashew nuts
pinch of salt
7.5 ml/1½ tsp lemon juice
fresh mint leaves,
    to garnish

1 Prepare the vegetables: cut the carrot, peppers and courgette into matchsticks, halve the beans and chop the spring onions. Set aside.

2 Heat the oil in a non-stick wok or frying pan and fry the curry leaf, cumin seeds and dried chilli for about 1 minute.

3 Add the vegetables and nuts and stir them around gently. Add the salt and lemon juice. Continue to stir and cook for about 3–5 minutes.

4 Transfer to a serving dish, garnish with mint leaves and serve.

COOK'S TIP: If you are very short of time, use frozen mixed vegetables, which also work well in this dish.

Herby Wild Rice Pilaf

A nutritious one-pot meal.

Serves 1

INGREDIENTS
50 g/2 oz/⅓ cup mixed brown basmati
    and wild rice
5 ml/1 tsp olive oil
½ small onion, chopped
1 garlic clove, crushed
2.5 ml/½ tsp ground cumin
2.5 ml/½ tsp ground turmeric
30 ml/2 tbsp sultanas
175 ml/6 fl oz/¾ cup vegetable stock
15 ml/1 tbsp chopped fresh mixed herbs
salt and freshly ground black pepper
fresh herb sprigs and 15 ml/1 tbsp pistachio
    nuts, to garnish

1 Wash the rice in a sieve under cold running water, then drain well. Heat the oil in a saucepan, add the onion and garlic and cook gently for 5 minutes, stirring occasionally.

2 Add the spices and rice and cook gently for 1 minute, stirring. Stir in the sultanas and stock, bring to the boil, cover and simmer for 20–25 minutes, until almost all the liquid has been absorbed, stirring occasionally.

3 Stir in the chopped herbs and season to taste with salt and pepper. Spoon the pilaf into a warmed bowl and garnish with herb sprigs and pistachio nuts.

Roast Baby Vegetables

Serve with black olives, if liked.

Serves 1

INGREDIENTS
165 g/5½ oz mixed baby vegetables, such as
    aubergine, onion or shallot, courgette,
    sweetcorn and button mushrooms
½ small red pepper, seeded and cut into
    large pieces
1 garlic clove, finely chopped
5 ml/1 tsp olive oil
5 ml/1 tsp chopped fresh mixed herbs
2–3 cherry tomatoes
60 ml/4 tbsp coarsely grated
    Mozzarella cheese
salt and freshly ground black pepper
black olives, to serve (optional)

1 Preheat the oven to 220°C/425°F/ Gas 7. Cut all the mixed baby vegetables in half lengthways.

2 Place the baby vegetables and pepper in a dish with the garlic and seasoning. Drizzle the oil over and toss the vegetables to coat them. Bake for 20 minutes, stirring once.

3 Remove the dish from the oven and stir in the herbs. Add the tomatoes and top with the Mozzarella. Bake for 5–10 minutes more.

Right: Herby Wild Rice Pilaf (top); Roast Baby Vegetables

Thai Noodles with Chinese Chives

This recipe requires a little time for preparation, but everything is cooked speedily in a hot wok and should be eaten at once.

Serves 1

INGREDIENTS
75 g/3 oz dried rice noodles
1.5 ml/¼ tsp grated fresh root ginger
7.5 ml/1½ tsp light soy sauce
12.5 ml/2½ tsp vegetable oil
50 g/2 oz Quorn, cut into small cubes
1 garlic clove, crushed
1 small onion, cut into thin wedges
25 g/1 oz fried bean curd, thinly sliced
1 small green chilli, seeded and finely sliced
50 g/2 oz beansprouts
25 g/1 oz Chinese chives, cut into
    5 cm/2 in lengths
30 ml/2 tbsp roasted peanuts,
    coarsely ground
7.5 ml/1½ tsp dark soy sauce
7.5 ml/1½ tsp chopped fresh coriander

1 Place the noodles in a bowl, cover with warm water and soak for 20–30 minutes, then drain. Blend together the ginger, light soy sauce and 5 ml/ 1 tsp of the oil in a bowl. Stir in the Quorn and set aside for 10 minutes. Drain, reserving the marinade.

2 Heat 5 ml/1 tsp of the oil in a wok or frying pan and fry the garlic for a few seconds. Add the Quorn and stir-fry for 2–3 minutes. Then transfer to a plate and set aside.

3 Heat the remaining oil in the wok or frying pan and stir-fry the onion wedges for 3–4 minutes, until softened and tinged with brown. Add the fried bean curd and chilli, stir-fry briefly and then add the noodles. Stir-fry for 4–5 minutes.

4 Stir in the beansprouts, Chinese chives and most of the ground peanuts, reserving a little for the garnish. Stir well, then add the Quorn, the dark soy sauce and the reserved marinade. Continue cooking for a further 1–2 minutes.

5 When hot, spoon on to a serving plate and garnish with the remaining ground peanuts and coriander.

VARIATION: Quorn makes this a vegetarian meal; however, thinly sliced pork or chicken could be used instead. Stir-fry it initially for 4–5 minutes.

Capellini with Rocket

A light but filling pasta dish with the added pepperiness of fresh rocket, the crispness of mangetouts and the crunchiness of pine nuts.

Serves 1

INGREDIENTS
65 g/2½ oz dried capellini or angel
   hair pasta
50 g/2 oz mangetouts
65 g/2½ oz rocket
15 ml/1 tbsp pine
   nuts, roasted
12.5 ml/2½ tsp finely grated
   Parmesan cheese
12.5 ml/2½ tsp olive oil

1 Cook the capellini or angel hair pasta, following the instructions on the packet, until *al dente*.

2 Top and tail the mangetouts and separate the rocket leaves.

3 As soon as the pasta is cooked, drop in the rocket and mangetouts, then drain immediately.

4 Toss the pasta in a large bowl with the roasted pine nuts, Parmesan and olive oil. Serve at once.

Tomato & Fennel Pizza

This pizza relies on the winning combination of tomatoes, fennel and Parmesan. The fennel adds both a crisp texture and a distinctive flavour.

Serves 1

INGREDIENTS
½ small fennel bulb
22.5 ml/4½ tsp olive oil
1 ready-made pizza base,
    20–25 cm/8–10 in diameter
250 ml/8 fl oz/1 cup ready-made
    tomato sauce
15 ml/1 tbsp chopped fresh
    flat leaf parsley
25 g/1 oz/¼ cup grated
    Mozzarella cheese
25 g/1 oz/⅓ cup grated
    Parmesan cheese
salt and freshly ground
    black pepper

1 Preheat the oven to 220°C/425°F/ Gas 7. Trim and slice the fennel lengthways. Remove the core and slice the remaining fennel thinly.

2 Heat 10 ml/2 tsp of the olive oil in a frying pan and sauté the fennel for 4–5 minutes, until just tender. Season.

3 Brush the pizza base with the remaining oil and spread over the tomato sauce. Spoon the fennel on top and scatter over the flat leaf parsley.

4 Mix together the Mozzarella and Parmesan and sprinkle over. Bake for 15 minutes, until crisp and golden. Serve immediately.

Cooked Vegetable Gado-Gado

This tasty Indonesian dish of mixed vegetables, bean curd and hard-boiled egg makes a filling supper. Omit the prawn crackers for vegetarians.

Serves 1

INGREDIENTS
75 g/3 oz mixed cabbage, spinach and
   beansprouts, rinsed and shredded
2.5 cm/1 in piece of cucumber cut in
   wedges, salted and set aside for
   15 minutes
1 egg, hard-boiled and shelled
25 g/1 oz bean curd
oil, for frying
2–3 prawn crackers (optional)
50 g/2 oz waxy potatoes, cooked
   and diced
lemon juice
deep-fried onions, to garnish (optional)

FOR THE PEANUT SAUCE
1 fresh red chilli, seeded and ground
150 ml/¼ pint/⅔ cup coconut milk
175 g/6 oz crunchy peanut butter
7.5 ml/1½ tsp dark soy sauce or
   dark brown sugar
22.5 ml/4½ tsp lemon juice
coarsely crushed peanuts
salt

1 First, make the peanut sauce. Put the chilli, coconut milk and peanut butter in a pan and heat gently, stirring until smooth. Simmer gently until thickened, then stir in the soy sauce or sugar and lemon juice. Season with salt to taste, pour into a bowl and stir in a few crushed peanuts. Set aside.

2 Bring a large pan of salted water to the boil. Plunge one type of raw vegetable at a time, except the cucumber, into the pan for just a few seconds to blanch. Lift out with a slotted spoon and run under very cold water. Drain thoroughly.

3 Rinse the cucumber pieces and drain them well. Cut the egg in quarters. Cut the bean curd into cubes.

4 Fry the bean curd in hot oil in a wok until crisp on both sides. Lift out and drain on kitchen paper.

5 Add more oil to the pan and then deep-fry the prawn crackers, if using. Drain on kitchen paper.

COOK'S TIP: Any leftover peanut sauce can be served with grilled chicken to make chicken satay.

6 Arrange all the cooked vegetables, including the potatoes, on a plate, with the cucumber, hard-boiled egg and bean curd. Sprinkle with the lemon juice and scatter over the fried onions, if using. Serve with the peanut sauce and prawn crackers, if using.

Cracked Wheat Salad

Subtle and unusual flavours are combined in this delicious salad.

Serves 1

INGREDIENTS
75 ml/5 tbsp vegetable stock
¼ cinnamon stick
pinch of ground cumin
pinch of ground cloves
pinch of salt
50 g/2 oz/¼ cup cracked wheat
6 mangetouts, topped and tailed
½ small red and ½ small yellow pepper,
    roasted, peeled, seeded and diced
1 small plum tomato, peeled,
    seeded and diced
1 small shallot, finely sliced
2 black olives, stoned and cut into quarters
7.5 ml/1½ tsp each shredded fresh basil,
    mint and parsley
7.5 ml/1½ tsp chopped walnuts
7.5 ml/1½ tsp balsamic vinegar
30 ml/2 tbsp extra virgin olive oil
freshly ground black pepper
onion rings, to garnish

1 Put the stock, spices and salt into a saucepan bring to the boil and cook for 1 minute.

2 Place the cracked wheat in a bowl, pour over the stock and leave to stand for 30 minutes.

3 In another bowl, mix together the mangetouts, peppers, tomato, shallot, olives, herbs and walnuts. Add the vinegar, olive oil and a little black pepper and stir thoroughly to mix.

COOK'S TIP: To roast the peppers, cut in half and place skin side up on a baking tray. Place in an oven preheated to 220°C/425°F/Gas 7 and roast for 20 minutes. Place in a plastic bag for 10 minutes. The skin will then be easily removed.

VARIATION: This salad lends itself to many variations. You could use French beans instead of mangetouts and substitute sun-dried tomatoes for the fresh ones. Other nuts, such as almonds, would also be delicious.

4 Strain the cracked wheat of any liquid and discard the cinnamon stick. Transfer to a plate, stir in the fresh vegetable mixture and serve, garnished with onion rings.

Plum, Rum & Raisin Brûlée

Crack through the crunchy caramel to find the juicy plums and smooth creamy centre of this dessert.

Serves 1

INGREDIENTS
15 ml/1 tbsp raisins
10 ml/2 tsp dark rum
75 g/3 oz medium plums
15 ml/1 tbsp orange juice
5 ml/1 tsp clear honey
50 g/2 oz/¼ cup soft cheese
30 ml/2 tbsp sugar

2 Quarter the plums and remove their stones. Put into a heavy-based saucepan, together with the orange juice and honey. Simmer gently for 5 minutes, or until soft. Stir in the soaked raisins. Reserve 5 ml/1 tsp of the juice, then transfer the remainder with the plums and raisins into a 150 ml/¼ pint/⅔ cup ramekin dish.

1 Put the raisins into a small bowl and sprinkle over the rum. Leave to soak for 5 minutes.

VARIATION: Simmer a large cooking apple with 25 g/1 oz sugar. Purée, then beat into 15 g/½ oz/ 1 tbsp butter. Add a dash of Calvados and chill before finishing as in Step 4.

3 Blend the soft cheese with the reserved plum juice. Spoon over the plums and raisins and chill in the fridge for 1 hour.

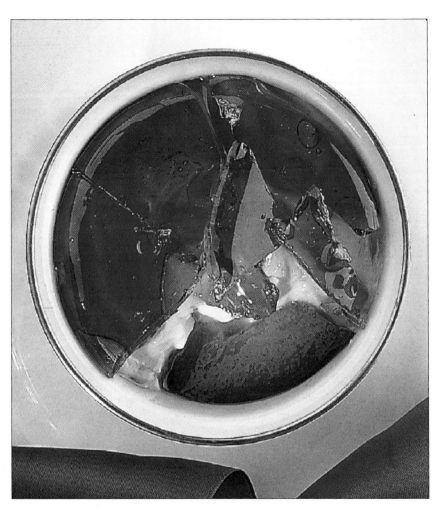

4 Put the sugar into a heavy-based saucepan with 15 ml/1 tbsp cold water. Heat gently, stirring, until the sugar has dissolved. Boil for about 10 minutes, or until it turns golden brown. Cool for 2 minutes, then carefully pour over the ramekin. Cool and serve.

Fruit Fondue with Hazelnut Dip

Fresh fruit is tasty, easy and good for you, but can become boring. Liven it up with this creamy dip.

Serves 1

INGREDIENTS
selection of fresh fruits for dipping,
    such as satsuma, kiwi fruit,
    grapes, strawberries and physalis
30 ml/2 tbsp soft cheese
75 ml/5 tbsp hazelnut yogurt
2.5 ml/½ tsp vanilla essence
2.5 ml/½ tsp caster sugar
30 ml/2 tbsp chopped hazelnuts

1 First prepare the fruits. Peel and segment the satsuma. Then peel the kiwi fruit and cut into wedges. Wash the grapes and strawberries. Peel back the papery casing on the physalis.

2 Beat the soft cheese with the yogurt, vanilla essence and sugar in a bowl. Stir in half the hazelnuts. Spoon into a small bowl and scatter over the remaining hazelnuts. Arrange the prepared fruits around the dip and serve immediately.

Right: Yogurt Sundae with Passion Fruit Coulis (top); Fruit Fondue with Hazelnut Dip

Yogurt Sundae with Passion Fruit Coulis

Give yourself a treat with all the flavour of homemade ice cream.

Serves 1

INGREDIENTS
75 g/3 oz strawberries, hulled and halved
1 small passion fruit, halved
2.5 ml/½ tsp icing sugar (optional)
1 small ripe peach, stoned and chopped
2 scoops vanilla or strawberry frozen yogurt
fresh mint sprigs, to garnish

1 Purée half the strawberries. Scoop out the passion fruit pulp and add it to the coulis. Sweeten, if necessary.

2 Spoon half the remaining strawberries and half the chopped peach into a sundae glass. Top with a scoop of frozen yogurt. Add a further layer of fruit, saving a few pieces for decoration, and another scoop of yogurt. Pour over the coulis and top with the pieces of fruit and mint.

Banana with Caribbean Coffee Sauce

This melt-in-the-mouth dessert has a magical flavour created by setting light to the rum.

Serves 1

INGREDIENTS
1 large banana
15 g/½ oz/1 tbsp butter
15 ml/1 tbsp soft dark brown sugar
15 ml/1 tbsp strong brewed coffee
15 ml/1 tbsp dark rum
vanilla ice cream, to serve

1 Peel the banana and cut in half lengthways. Melt the butter in a large frying pan over a medium heat. Add the banana and cook for 3 minutes, turning halfway through cooking time.

2 Sprinkle the sugar over the banana, then add the coffee. Continue cooking, stirring occasionally, for 2–3 minutes, or until the banana is tender.

3 Pour the rum into the pan and bring to the boil. With a long match or taper and tilting the pan, ignite the rum. As soon as the flames subside, serve the banana immediately with vanilla ice cream.

Right: Banana with Caribbean Coffee Sauce (top); Nectarine with Coffee Mascarpone

Nectarine with Coffee Mascarpone

This simple dessert is perfect for nectarines that are still slightly hard and under-ripe.

Serves 1

INGREDIENTS
25 g/1 oz/2 tbsp Mascarpone cheese
10 ml/2 tsp cold very strong
   brewed coffee
1 nectarine
5 ml/1 tsp melted butter
10 ml/2 tsp clear honey
pinch of ground mixed spice
15 ml/1 tbsp slivered Brazil nuts

1 Beat the Mascarpone to soften then mix in the coffee. Cover with clear film and chill for 20 minutes.

2 Cut the nectarine in half and remove the stone. Mix the butter, 5 ml/1 tsp of the honey and spice. Brush the cut surfaces with the butter.

3 Place the nectarine in a foil-lined grill pan. Cook under a hot grill for 2–3 minutes. Add the Brazil nuts to the grill pan for the last minute of cooking. Put a spoonful of the cheese mixture in the centre of each nectarine half. Drizzle with the remaining honey and sprinkle with the toasted Brazil nuts before serving.

Apple Pancakes

These pancakes are filled with cinnamon-spiced caramelized apples.

Serves 1

INGREDIENTS
50 g/2 oz/½ cup plain flour
pinch of salt
1 egg, beaten
75 ml/5 tbsp milk
60 ml/4 tbsp water
15 g/½ oz/1 tbsp butter, melted
sunflower oil, for frying
cinnamon sugar or icing sugar and lemon
    wedges, to serve (optional)

FOR THE FILLING
20 g/¾ oz/1½ tbsp butter
225 g/8 oz eating apples, cored, peeled
    and sliced
10 ml/2 tsp caster sugar
1.5 ml/¼ tsp ground cinnamon

1 Melt the butter for the filling in a heavy-based frying pan. When the foam subsides, add the apples, sugar and cinnamon. Cook, stirring occasionally for 8–10 minutes, until the apples are soft and golden brown. Set aside and keep warm.

2 Sift the flour and salt into a mixing bowl and make a well in the middle. Add the egg and gradually mix in the flour from the sides.

3 Slowly add the combined milk and water, beating until smooth. Stir in the melted butter.

4 Heat 10 ml/2 tsp oil in a crêpe or small frying pan. Pour in about 30 ml/2 tbsp of the batter, tipping the pan to coat the base evenly.

5 Cook the pancake until the underside is golden brown, then turn over and cook the other side. Slide on to a warm plate, cover with foil and set the plate over a pan of simmering water to keep warm. Repeat with the remaining batter mixture, until it is all used up (see Cook's Tip).

6 Divide the apple filling between two pancakes and roll them up. Sprinkle with cinnamon sugar or icing sugar, if liked. Serve with lemon wedges.

COOK'S TIP: This is the smallest convenient quantity of pancake batter, but will be more than is required for one serving. Cook pancakes until all the batter is used up and stack them, interleaved with greaseproof paper. When cold, wrap the uneaten pancakes in a plastic freezer bag and freeze for up to three months. They can be used individually, will thaw in just a few moments and may be filled or topped with either a savoury or sweet filling.

This edition is published by Hermes House, an imprint of Anness Publishing Ltd,
Hermes House, 88–89 Blackfriars Road, London SE1 8HA;
tel. 020 7401 2077; fax 020 7633 9499

www.hermeshouse.com; www.annesspublishing.com

If you like the images in this book and would like to investigate using them for publishing, promotions
or advertising, please visit our website www.practicalpictures.com for more information.

Publisher: Joanna Lorenz
Editor: Valerie Ferguson
Series Designer: Bobbie Colgate Stone
Designer: Andrew Heath
Editorial Reader: Penelope Goodare
Production Controller: Joanna King

Recipes contributed by: Catherine Atkinson, Carla Capalbo, Lesley Chamberlain, Maxine Clarke,
Carole Clements, Trisha Davies, Roz Denny, Patrizia Diemling, Matthew Drennan, Sarah Edmonds, Joanna Farrow,
Christine France, Shirley Gill, Nicola Graimes, Deh-Ta Hsiung, Shehzad Husain, Christine Ingram, Judy Jackson,
Sallie Morris, Annie Nichols, Maggie Pannell, Anne Sheasby, Liz Trigg, Hilaire Walden, Laura Washburn,
Steven Wheeler, Elizabeth Wolf-Cohen.

Photography: Karl Adamson, Edward Allwright, Steve Baxter, Louise Dove, Mickie Dowie,
James Duncan, Ian Garlick, Michelle Garrett, Amanda Heywood, Ferguson Hill, Janine Hosegood,
David Jordan, Don Last, William Lingwood, Patrick McLeavey, Thomas Odulate.

ETHICAL TRADING POLICY
Because of our ongoing ecological investment programme, you, as our customer, can have the pleasure and
reassurance of knowing that a tree is being cultivated on your behalf to naturally replace the materials used to make
the book you are holding. For further information about this scheme, go to www.annesspublishing.com/trees

Notes:
For all recipes, quantities are given in both metric and imperial measures and, where appropriate, measures are also
given in standard cups and spoons.
Follow one set, but not a mixture, because they are not interchangeable.
Standard spoon and cup measures are level.
1 tsp = 5 ml   1 tbsp = 15 ml
1 cup = 250 ml/8 fl oz
Australian standard tablespoons are 20 ml. Australian readers should use 3 tsp in place of
1 tbsp for measuring small quantities of gelatine, cornflour, salt, etc.
Medium eggs are used unless otherwise stated.